A Color Guide to Corn Snakes

Captive-Bred in th

by Michael J. McEachern

Table of Contents

Introduction 2

General Information 3

Mutations That Affect the Color of Corn Snakes 11

Mutations That Affect the Pattern of Corn Snakes 18

Combinations of Mutations 28

Non-Heritable Alterations of Corn Snake Appearance 32

Hybridization of Corn Snakes with Other Species 35

Appendix: Genetics Primer 36

Glossary of Corn Snake Varieties 47

Introduction

The attractive appearance, mild disposition, and ready acclimation to captivity have helped make the North American corn snake *(Elaphe guttata)* one of the most abundant species of reptile kept in captivity. Another feature of corn snakes that contributes to their popularity as captive specimens is their considerable variety. Wild populations of corn snakes naturally exhibit a substantial degree of variation in their coloration . In recent years, this variation has been significantly supplemented by the selective breeding of animals with mutations that affect color and pattern.

This book is intended to describe and illustrate examples of the known varieties of corn snakes, both those seen in the wild and those seen only in captivity. Also provided is an Appendix describing basic genetic terms and principles relevant to understanding the inheritance of corn snake traits. Some readers may wish to read through the Appendix before reading the sections dealing with mutations affecting corn snakes. Information on the care and husbandry of corn snakes in captivity is provided in the companion book "Keeping and Breeding Corn Snakes" by the same author.

A "creamsicle" (top) and an amelanistic (bottom) corn snake. Photo by the author.

General Information

WHAT IS AND WHAT ISN'T A CORN SNAKE

The animals that are described in this book are all members of the species *Elaphe guttata,* more commonly known as the corn snake. Members of the genus *Elaphe*, including the corn snake, are often referred to as rat snakes because of their tendency to feed on rodents. Indeed, another common name used for the corn snake is "red rat snake". Occasionally, one may also see the name corn snake attached to other snake species, such as "Chinese corn snake", as a means of giving a familiar sounding name to an unfamiliar species. While these other species may be attractive and interesting animals and, may in fact be related to corn snakes, they are not corn snakes. Only representatives of the North American species *Elaphe guttata* are true corn snakes.

A more common confusion comes from true corn snakes going by names other than corn snake. Not only is the name red rat snake used for corn snakes, but the name "Great Plains rat snake" and "rosy rat snake" are used as the common names for different subspecies of the corn snake. Despite the lack of "corn" in their names, the Great Plains rat snake and the rosy rat snake are full fledged corn snakes belonging to the species *Elaphe guttata.*

Although currently rare, a likely source of some future confusion are hybrids between corn snakes and certain related snakes, including gopher snakes, king snakes, and other rat snakes. The names given to these hybrid animals by the breeders that produced them and who are trying to market them may well include the word "corn" in them. "Jungle corn" is one such name that I have heard of. Being hybrids between different species, these animals are obviously not true corn snakes.

DESCRIPTION OF THE SPECIES

Corn snakes are constrictors that prey upon a variety of small vertebrates in the wild and are typically fed mice in captivity. Adult corn snakes are typically two and a half to five feet (76-152 cm) in length with a maximum recorded length of six feet (183 cm). The markings of corn snakes are characterized by a series of prominent blotches that run down the center of the backs (dorsal blotches) along with smaller blotches that run along both sides (lateral blotches). The head is distinctively marked with a pair of stripes, one running through the eyes, and the other on top of the head, that merge near the front to produce an "arrowhead" of the same color as the dorsal blotches. The stripes on top of the head connect with the first blotch on the back of the neck. The natural coloration of corn snakes is highly variable. Ground color may be gray, brown, or orange and blotches may be red-orange or brown. The blotches are typically darker and/or redder than the ground color and are usually outlined in black and sometimes additionally with a little white. Sometimes, four wide dullish stripes may be faintly visible running down the back on top of the blotched pattern. The belly of corn snakes are typically marked with bold black checks on a white and/or orange background that turn into black stripes on the underside of the tail.   In some individuals, the checks may be mostly orange or may be largely absent. Corn snakes are fairly slender snakes which, along with other North American rat snakes, have a body cross section shaped rather like a loaf of bread instead of the more round cross section seen with most snakes. The scales of corn snakes are smooth or slightly keeled, and the anal scale is divided. There are typically 25 to 35 rows of scales at midbody.

Baby corn snakes hatch out of eggs at 8-15 inches (20-38 cm) in length. Their patterns are essentially the same as those of adults, but their coloration is often rather different, being characterized by less orange and by higher contrast in their markings.

SOURCES OF VARIETY IN CORN SNAKES

By variety, I refer of course to variety in the appearance of the animals. Variety in other traits of corn snakes such as size and temperament also exist, but it is differences in appearance that are most noticed and that are most likely to appeal to people interested in keeping and breeding corn snakes. The sources of variation in corn snake appearance are given below:

1. Variation in appearance between juveniles and adults.
2. Natural appearance differences that exist between different subspecies of corn snakes.
3. Natural variation in appearance that occurs within a given subspecies of corn snake.
4. Natural or selectively bred hybridization between different subspecies.
5. Mutations that affect coloration.
6. Mutations that affect pattern.
7. Combinations of two or more color or pattern mutations.
8. Combinations of a mutation affecting appearance with naturally occurring variation.
9. Non-heritable abnormalities affecting appearance.
10. Hybridization with related snake species.

Examples of each of these sources of variety are discussed in this book. Not included in the above list, because of its temporary nature, is the fading of color associated with the days prior to skin shedding.

JUVENILE VERSUS ADULT COLORATION

Corn snakes, at least of the eastern subspecies, hatch out with darker blotches and less red-orange coloration than are present in adults and show distinctly less variation in appearance between individuals than is seen in adult corn snakes.

4

Gradually, as the animals mature, their coloration will change to the colorations typical of adult corn snakes. In some individuals, especially those destined to have lots of orange and not very much black, the coloration changes that occur with growth are considerable. Color changes are much less apparent once corn snakes have reached maturity although the markings of many individuals have a tendency to darken and lose contrast as they age. The color of adult amelanistic corn snakes can sometimes fade somewhat with age.

Although it is impossible to say for sure what a hatchling corn snake will look like as an adult, one can make a pretty good guess on the basis of what its parents look like and by how the hatchling looks relative to other hatchlings.

SUBSPECIES OF THE CORN SNAKE

Two subspecies of *Elaphe guttata* are universally recognized and a third subspecies is sometimes still referred to. However, the validity of the third subspecies, *Elaphe guttata rosacea*, has been cast in doubt by some recent studies.

By far, the predominant subspecies in captive collections is *Elaphe guttata guttata* which occurs naturally in the southeastern United States and which is referred to as the **red rat snake**, or more typically, simply called the **corn snake**.

In the south central United States and in north eastern Mexico lives *Elaphe guttata emoryi*, the subspecies of corn snake also known as the **Great Plains rat snake**. This subspecies differs from the eastern subspecies by a near complete lack of red or orange pigmentation. E. g. emoryi are grey or brown animals with darker brown blotches. Some orange coloration may be visible on the belly or in the irises of the eyes. Other differences that can be present in this subspecies include larger head size, larger eye size in relation to the head, a greater number of dorsal blotches, a diminished amount of black on the belly, and fewer, but larger eggs laid by the females. Record length for this subspecies, five feet (152 cm), is rather less than the record length for *E. g. guttata*.

The third possible subspecies of the corn snake is *Elaphe guttata rosacea*, otherwise known as the **rosy rat snake**. These animals are similar to *Elaphe guttata guttata* except for largely lacking black markings on both their dorsal or ventral surfaces. Rosy rat snakes live in the lower Florida Keys and were originally identified by Cope in 1888 as a separate species, on the basis of a single specimen. Two investigators reduced it to the status of a subspecies of the corn snake around 1950, and a majority of the few subsequent studies have favored not even considering it as a separate subspecies.

VARIATION WITHIN A SUBSPECIES

In addition to the variation that exists between the subspecies of corn snakes, there can be considerable natural variation even within a single subspecies. This is best

The corn snake *(Elaphe guttata guttata)* . Photo by Bill Love

Great Plains rat snake *(Elaphe emoryi)*. Photo by the author.

Rosy rat snake *(Elaphe guttata rosacea)*. Photo by Bill Love.

Ventral surface of rosy rat snake. Photo by Bill Love.

7

known for *Elaphe guttata guttata* where different individuals of this subspecies are often highly different in appearance. This variation within a subspecies, like the variation between subspecies, is largely or entirely heritable as mating similar looking corn snakes together will produce offspring that will grow to resemble the parents.

Often, different geographic areas tend to produce different looking corn snakes. Conant and Collins (1991, Peterson Field Guide Series, Houghton Mifflin Co., Boston), for example, describe corn snakes from some upland areas as tending toward browns. Often, specimens of *Elaphe guttata guttata* may be sold under the names "Okeetee" corn snake and "Miami phase" corn snake, both of which refer to geographic areas.

The name **"Okeetee"** corn snake seems to have spread from Carl Kauffeld's description (in the 1957 book "Snakes and Snake Hunting" (Hanover House) and the 1969 book "Snakes: The Keeper and the Kept" (Doubleday & Co., Inc., Garden City, NY)) of the particularly handsome corn snakes seen on land owned by a hunting plantation named the The Okeetee Club in Jasper County in southern South Carolina. In current use, the name Okeetee is often simply used to mean wild-type corn snakes that are particularly rich in orange coloration, regardless of their geographic origin. Although certain geographic areas may tend to produce corn snakes with particular appearance traits, there can be considerable differences in the appearance of animals even at a single locale. Handsome orange corn snakes, for example, are not limited to South Carolina and corn snakes from Okeetee are not necessarily especially attractive.

"Miami phase" is a name that has been coined for corn snakes that have a grey ground color and have black-edged red-orange blotches. Many animals like this occur in the area of Miami, Florida. Nice examples of this variety of corn snake can easily rival their more orange-colored kin in attractiveness, but are currently rather uncommon in captive collections. Like "Okeetee", the name "Miami phase" refers foremost to appearance traits and will not necessarily indicate that the animal originated near Miami.

A Miami phase female that I have owned for many years is a small shy animal that lays smaller than average eggs and produces babies more prone than average to initially insist on lizards for meals. Some of these characteristics are probably typical of this phase of corn snake.

"Okeetee" corn snake. Photo by Bill Love.

"Miami phase" corn snake. Photo by the author.

HYBRIDIZATION BETWEEN SUBSPECIES

The different subspecies of corn snake can be successfully bred to one another. The offspring of a mating between a *E. g. guttata* and an *E. g. emoryi* will look rather intermediate between the two parents. They will be much more brown than eastern corn snakes *(E. g. guttata)* normally are, yet have a pronounced underlying orange tinge that is absent in *E. g. emoryi*. The corn snakes of certain areas, especially in parts of northern Louisiana, have features intermediate between the two subspecies and presumably represent a population that are natural hybrids (intergrades) between the two subspecies.

Crossing *E. g. emoryi* to *E. g. guttata* individuals that carry the mutation for amelanism (lack of the black pigment melanin) has helped produce amelanistic corn snakes that are particularly light orange in color (see "creamsicle" corn snake in the section concerning amelanism). In addition to producing variety in appearance among captive corn snake populations, hybridizations may help serve to introduce desirable traits of one subspecies into the other. For example, at least some *E. g. emoryi* females produce hatchlings that are much larger in size and that can be particularly easy to start feeding relative to the hatchlings of *E. g. guttata* females. Large hatchling size could be a trait that some would find desirable to have present in *E. g. guttata*.

Hybrid Great Plains rat snake *(Elaphe g. emoryi)* x corn snake *(Elaphe g. guttata)*. Photo by the author.

Mutations That Affect the Color of Corn Snakes

Among the most important sources of the variation in the appearance of corn snakes kept in captivity are mutations that affect coloration. There currently are at least three known mutations that alter the color of corn snakes. In each case, the mutation causes either a diminishment or a complete loss of one of the pigments normally present in the skin of corn snakes. All three mutations are recessive, needing to be homozygous in order to have any effect.

AMELANISM

By far, the most common mutation seen in captive corn snakes is the mutation that causes amelanism, the absence of the pigment melanin. Amelanism has been recorded in a wide variety of animal species, including many other snake species. In mammals, amelanism is the equivalent of albinism because melanins are the only type of pigment that contribute to skin, hair, and eye color. Amelanistic mammals are thus true albinos, lacking all external pigmentation. Amelanistic corn snakes, though often referred to as albinos (or sometimes as "red albinos"), retain other pigments in their skin and are not considered true albinos. The loss of the black, brown, and grey coloration produced by melanin produces a corn snake that has red eyes and strikingly bright red orange body coloration. The pattern of markings on the animals remains essentially unaffected, although the absence of dark pigment may render features that are normally black, such as the ventral checks, nearly invisible.

The first recorded amelanistic corn snake was a male captured in Stanley county North Carolina in 1953 which was maintained at the Children's Nature Museum in Charlotte until 1959. It was then loaned to H. Bernard Bechtel and Elizabeth Bechtel of Valdosta, Georgia for breeding purposes. That year, the amelanistic male was successfully bred to three normal female corn snakes producing 46 normal looking hatchlings. In 1961, some of these hatchlings were bred to one another resulting in the production of a number of amelanistic hatchlings, thereby demonstrating the heritable nature of the amelanistic trait. The original amelanistic male died only months after the 1959 breedings, yet he is believed to be the forefather of most of the amelanistic corn snakes now in existence. In subsequent years there have been numerous other amelanistic corn snakes caught in the wild in a number of states, and a few of these have also left many captive descendants.

Amelanism in corn snakes is caused by a single recessive mutation. An animal must carry the mutation in the homozygous state (i. e., both copies of the relevant gene must be mutated) in order for the animal to be amelanistic. All amelanism in corn snakes appears to involve the same gene. This means that breeding together any two amelanistic corn snakes will produce all amelanistic offspring. In some

11

Amelanistic corn snake with "Miami phase" background. Photo by the author.

An orange amelanistic corn snake with little white on the dorsal surface. Photo by Bill Love.

A "Reverse Okeetee" amelanistic corn snake selectively-bred by Glades Herpetoculture. Photo by Bill Love.

"Creamsicle" corn snake. Photo by Mark Bell.

species, more than one type of amelanism exists and breeding two amelanistic individuals will not guarantee that amelanistic offspring will be produced. One way of categorizing amelanism is through the presence or absence in the skin of tyrosinase, an enzyme which is involved in the synthesis of melanin. In some other animal species, including humans, both tyrosinase minus and tyrosinase positive amelanistic mutations exist. Amelanistic corn snakes lack tyrosinase activity in their skin and are classified as tyrosinase minus.

Amelanistic corn snakes, like wild type corn snakes, show a substantial degree of variation in color. They can have deep red orange blotches on a light orange or pink ground color. They can be a nearly solid, bright orange. They can have deep red orange blotches on a light orange or pink ground color. These high contrast animals have been called "candy corns". When crossed into the *E. g. emoryi* subspecies, they can be relatively light orange or yellow-orange, a variation that has been coined **"Creamsicle"** corns. Most individuals are somewhere in between these extremes. Hatchling amelanistic corn snakes tend to be closer to their adult coloration than are hatchling wild type corns. Even so, amelanistic hatchlings tend to look more alike than do adult amelanistics and, like normally pigmented hatchlings, will generally acquire more orange pigmentation as they mature.

HYPOMELANISM

Hypomelanism is a genetic trait that has been found in a few snake species including corn snakes which distinctly reduces, but does not eliminate, the amount of melanin pigmentation present in the skin. In hypomelanistic corn snakes, the eyes remain black and the overall coloration tends to be intermediate between that of a normal corn snake and that of an amelanistic corn snake. Hypomelanistic animals can be fairly variable and can range from practically resembling a black eyed amelanistic animal to being dark enough to be readily mistaken for being a particularly light colored normal corn snake. Like amelanism, hypomelanism is inherited as a single recessive mutation and appears to involve a different gene than the one involved in amelanism.

The first hypomelanistic corn snake was wild caught in central Florida around 1984 and displayed at Reptile World in St. Cloud, Florida. Bill and Kathy Love of Alva, Florida acquired descendants of this animal and demonstrated that it was a heritable trait. At least one other hypomelanistic corn snake has subsequently been found (which breeds true with the original strain). At the time of this writing, hypomelanistic corn snakes are not very widespread, but their highly attractive appearance and simple inheritance will undoubtedly lead to them becoming more common.

Hypomelanistic corn snake. Photo by Bill Love.

ANERYTHRISM

This trait could be said to be the complement of amelanism. Instead of black being gone and orange still being present as is the case with amelanism, it is exactly the reverse in anerythristic corn snakes. Anerythristic corn snakes are marked with black, grey, and sometimes brown or yellow, but are missing red and orange and superficially resemble *Elaphe guttata emoryi*, the western subspecies of corn snake. The yellow pigmentation, when present, tends to be most noticeable along the sides of the head and neck. Anerythristic corn snakes are sometimes referred to as "black albinos" or sometimes, incorrectly, as melanistics. H. B. Bechtel recommends referring to them as "axanthic", as red is the principle pigment of cells known as xanthophores which are responsible for the red skin coloration in corn snakes. Typically, however, axanthic refers to animals missing yellow coloration (xanthos is Greek for yellow), and therefore axanthic may not be the best choice as a name.

Anerythristic corn snakes occur as a significant minority (perhaps as much as 10%) of certain wild populations of corn snakes in Florida, especially in the southern part of the state. They have also been recorded wild in Georgia and South Carolina. Anerythrism in corn snakes had been demonstrated to be a genetic trait by 1973, when Glen Slemmer reported combining amelanism and anerythrism to produce a white "snow" corn snake.

15

Subadult anerythrystic corn snake. Photo by the author.

Anerythristic corn snake. Photo by the author.

Until recently, it had been thought that all anerythristic corn snakes carried the same defective gene. However, a second type of anerythrism, involving a different gene, has recently been identified. This second type of anerythrism, which I will refer to as Type B anerythrism (and I will refer to the more common type as Type A anerythrism), originated with a wild caught female collected in 1984 on Pine Island in Lee County, Florida. This individual was unusual in that it lacked the yellow highlights generally seen in other anerythristics. Breeding experiments done in subsequent years by Bill and Kathy Love showed that crossing this animal with a typical anerythristic corn snake did not produce all anerythristic offspring as was expected. Type A anerythrism clearly is inherited as a single recessive gene. The limited available evidence suggests that this is also true of Type B anerythrism. Anerythristic offspring can be produced only if both parents carry a mutation for the same type of anerythrism. But because virtually all anerythristic corn snakes in captive populations are believed to be of the Type A variety, there should be little chance for "incompatibility" problems for people who wish to breed anerythristics. Type A anerythrism is not what causes the lack of orange of *Elaphe guttata emoryi* as breeding a Type A anerythristic *E. g. guttata* to an *E. g. emoryi* will produce offspring that have orange pigmentation. To my knowledge, it has not been verified whether this is also true of Type B anerythrism.

MELANISM

Another genetic trait that may possibly affect coloration in corn snakes is melanism. I say possibly because, although melanistic corn snakes have been reported seen, I am unaware of this trait having yet been shown to be genetic.

A melanistic animal is an animal that has much more black coloration than do typical members of its species. Often they will be entirely black. This is not the same as anerythrism, which is the absence of red and orange pigmentation. An anerythristic corn snake has little or no more black than does a normal corn snake. Conversely, a melanistic corn snake would presumably retain red pigmentation, but it might normally be totally or completely obscured by the extra black pigment. A melanistic corn snake was reported to have a black dorsal surface but still retain some of the white on the ventral surface. Though reputed to be in captivity, melanistic corn snakes have yet to surface in the herpetocultural mainstream.

Mutations That Affect the Pattern of Corn Snakes

The mutations described previously alter coloration but do not alter the pattern of corn snakes. However, several mutations exist that markedly affect pattern but do not affect coloration. Corn snakes carrying mutations that affect pattern are currently rather rare in captivity (and all but absent in the wild), but will undoubtedly become more common, and lower priced, as time goes on. All four known pattern mutations appear to be inherited as single recessive genes.

STRIPING

The striping mutation, of all known corn snake mutations, produces snakes that perhaps least resemble typical corn snakes. This mutation produces four longitudinal stripes in the place of the blotches that are normally present on the sides and backs of corn snakes. The dorsal blotches are replaced by two stripes that are often perfectly smooth sided over much of the length of the animal. Thin areas in the striping may be present anywhere along the body and gaps in the striping are typically present on and near the tail. The lateral blotches of striped corn snakes are also replaced on each side by other stripes, though these lateral stripes are more likely to resemble dashed lines. A small fraction of individuals carrying the striping trait will have some dorsal blotches present in the form of thin hourglass shapes connecting the two dorsal stripes. Additionally, the normal ventral pattern of checkered marks is completely absent. The arrowhead pattern on the head is still present, but may be partially disrupted and may not connect with the body stripes. The striped corn snakes that are currently available are very orange and often lack contrast in their markings. Further generations of breeding should be able to introduce the striping trait into animals with other colorations.

The striping mutation was first seen by Mike Nolan in England around 1985 as a result of the breeding of two siblings from wild caught parents. The parents, and some of the offspring were purchased by Ernie Wagner of Seattle, Washington, and his animals have been the source of most or all of the striped corn snakes that have been produced in the United States. To this point in time, there has been a significant problem with low fertility in male striped corn snakes. This problem may well disappear as striped corns are outcrossed (as seems to have happened with snow corns, which also originally seemed prone to male infertility). However, as Ernie Wagner has yet to see a fully fertile male striped corn snake, it remains conceivable that fertility problems are intrinsic to the striping mutation.

MOTLEY

The so-called "motley" mutation of corn snakes causes pattern abnormalities that can resemble those seen in the striping mutation. Like the striping mutation, the motley mutation eliminates the normal ventral pattern. Also like the striping

18

Close-up of a normal colored striped corn snake. Photo by the author.

Normal colored striped corn snakes. Photo by the author.

Amelanistic striped corn snake. Photo by Mark Bell.

Anerythristic striped corn snake. Photo by Mark Bell.

Striped "snow" corn snake. Photo by Mark Bell.

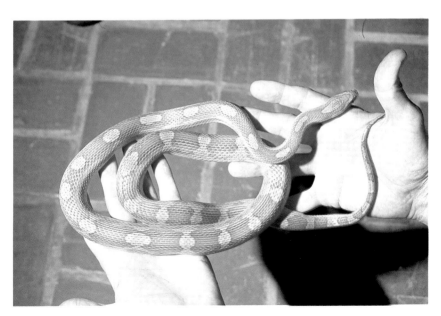

Dr. Bechthel's original "motley" corn snake. Photo by Bill Love.

Amelanistic "motley" corn snakes. Photo by Bill Love.

mutation, motley can produce longitudinal stripes. However, the stripes produced by this mutation typically only extend part of the length of the animal and are not nearly as smooth-sided as the stripes produced by the striping mutation. Instead, they are generally "bulged" in the places along the back where blotches would normally be. Along much of their length, motley corn snakes may have either normal looking blotches or blotches connected together by lateral striping. Overall, motley corn snakes give the impression of a pattern that couldn't "decide" if it wanted to be blotched or if it wanted to be striped.

Historically, the motley mutation dates back to a newly hatched female purchased in 1972 by H. Bernard Bechtel because of its unusual pattern. In 1977, this individual was crossed back to her own son (a son to daughter cross was also done), and the trait was demonstrated to be heritable.

VENTRAL PATTERN LOSS MUTATION OF BLOOD RED CORN SNAKES
Perhaps the least noticeable of the known corn snake mutations is one that, like the striping and motley mutations, eliminates the normal checkered pattern on the ventral surface. However, this mutation, which is found in **"blood red"** corn snakes, does not affect the dorsal blotches and is therefore less conspicuous. The

"Blood red" corn snake. Photo by Bill Love.

Anerythristic "blood red" corn snake. Photo by Mark Bell.

23

mutation possibly may also affect the lateral blotches, as these are generally absent or diminished in blood red corn snakes. The ventral pattern loss mutation is inherited as a recessive gene.

Currently, the ventral pattern loss mutation seems limited to being present in blood red corn snakes, a strain bred for being a rather solid dark red-orange in color and for lacking virtually all black pigmentation, except for in the eyes. The mutation that causes the loss of ventral pattern does not seem to contribute to the unusual coloration of blood red corns and it may have simply emerged from the inbreeding that was used to select for the attractive coloration of blood red corns. The pattern mutation is not the same as, and should not be confused with, the coloration trait.

ZIGZAG

The zigzag trait is a heritable trait that changes the regular pattern of dorsal blotches into one that generally includes long stretches of smaller dorsal blotches connected together, often in a wavy, zigzag pattern. The ventral pattern of zigzag corn snakes remains unchanged. The zigzag trait is quite variable, with some animals having a zigzag pattern down most of their length and with other animals having much less zigzagging. This variability has made determining the mode of inheritance somewhat difficult, but it appears that this trait is probably due to a single recessive mutation. The variability in the amount of zigzagging appears consistent with a simple model for how dorsal pattern in corn snakes develops (see next section).

The zigzag trait was first developed by Bill and Kathy Love from inbreeding animals descended from the original Pine Island (Type B) anerythristic corn snake.

"Zigzag" corn snake. Photo by Bill Love.

24

"Zigzag" corn snake. Photo by Bill Love.

Anerythristic "zigzag" corn snake. Photo by Mark Bell.

25

Combinations of Mutations

Through the appropriate breeding, it is possible to produce corn snakes that express two or more mutations that alter appearance. To date however, only a few of the many possible combinations of the known mutations have been produced. Two combinations of mutations that are the most widespread in captivity and that warrant particular attention here are the so-called "snow" corns and "ghost" corns.

SNOW CORN SNAKES

Snow corn is the most common name that has been given to corn snakes that are both amelanistic and anerythristic. This name stems from their whitish coloration combined with the fact that the term "albino" is generally reserved for corn snakes that carry only the trait for amelanism. Another name used occasionally for snow corn snakes is "white albino". This double mutant variety of corn snake is the most common mutant combination available.

Despite lacking two pigments, snow corns are still not true albinos as they have a visible pattern generally made up of whites, pinks, and yellows. Upon hatching, snow corn snakes are typically white animals with rather translucent pinkish blotches and no other coloration. As they mature, they lose their rather translucent look and often gradually gain some pink and/or yellow. As adults, individual snow corns snakes can display a fairly considerable degree of variation. They can be nearly solid white, white with off-white blotches, white with light yellow blotches, white with pink blotches or pinkish with yellow and pink blotches. Some are reputedly pink to the point of resembling amelanistics. I have even heard of some being described as having a greenish cast.

Because the snow corn "trait" is caused by a combination of two recessive mutations, its inheritance is more complicated than traits caused by single recessive mutations. Readers can refer to the Appendix for more information about this.

GHOST CORN SNAKES

"Ghost corn" is the name that has been coined for corn snakes that are both anerythristic and hypomelanistic. This combination of mutations results in snakes that lack red but that retain a modest amount of melanin pigmentation and consequently are generally rather tan in coloration. Like snow corns, they can have yellow and pinkish components to their coloration.

Additionally, there appears to be anerythristic corn snakes that are lightly pigmented in the manner of ghost corns but that are unrelated to the original ghost corn stock. These animals may possibly be due to the anerythrism mutation having been crossed into corn snakes that naturally have a greatly diminished amount of black pigment. This may mean that it perhaps is possible to breed two "ghost-like" corn snakes together and wind up with standard dark anerythristic offspring.

A "snow" corn snake with a strong yellow pattern. Photo by the author.

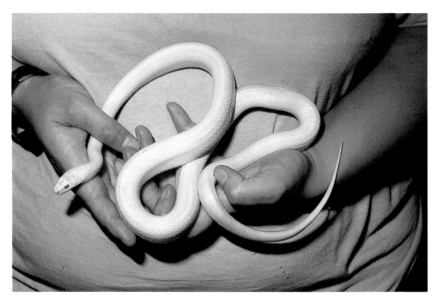
A "snow" corn snake with little pattern. Photo by Bill Love.

"Ghost" corn snake. Photo by Bill Love.

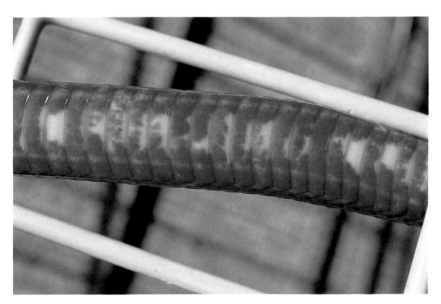

Ventral surface of "blood red" corn snake. Photo by the author.

COMBINING A MUTATION WITH NATURAL VARIATION

The considerable variation in coloration that is seen with wild corn snakes could, in principle, also be present among corn snakes expressing color or pattern mutations. Some of the extremes of variation in the different classes of mutant corn snakes have been described already in the sections pertaining to the particular mutation. A couple of "strains" that fit into this category and that are worth mentioning again here are the "blood red" corns and "creamsicle" corns.

BLOOD RED CORN SNAKES

Blood red corn snakes (sometimes shortened to just "blood corns") are characterized by two traits in particular. First, as mentioned earlier, they carry a recessive mutation that eliminates the checkered ventral pattern and largely eliminates the lateral blotches. Second, they are a rather solid, dark red-orange in coloration. Little or no black coloration is present either ventrally or dorsally, and uniformity of the red-orange coloration can largely obscure the blotched dorsal pattern. Hatchling blood red corns have white venters and are less orange and much more noticeably patterned than adults. With maturity, orange pigment is not only more prominent dorsally, but can spread to cover much of the underside in a rather irregular fashion. The color of blood red corns in clearly heritable but is not understood except to the point of saying that it is not due to a single gene.

Blood red corn snakes are a strain originally produced by Eddie Leach of Gainesville, Florida after a number of years of selective breeding. He began with wild-caught animals from a particular locale and inbred their descendants to produce what are now known as blood red corns.

Currently, blood red corns are a strain that appears to be somewhat negatively affected from inbreeding (see comments on inbreeding in the Appendix). A number of people with experience keeping them, including myself, have found them to grow and reproduce relatively poorly compared to most corn snakes. Additionally, they are distinctly more prone to be lizard eaters as hatchlings than are most other corn snakes. Unfortunately, the fact that the blood red corn traits are not inherited in simple fashion will not make it easy to outcross them and recover descendants with the original combination of traits. Only outcrossing, however, will allow the strain to regain some vigor.

CREAMSICLE CORN SNAKES

Creamsicle corn snakes, mentioned earlier in the section on amelanism, are corn snakes that are amelanistic and that have a considerable amount of genetic background from *E. g. emoryi*, the western subspecies of corn snake. The mutation combined with the decreased red-orange from the *E. g. emoryi* background result in an amelanistic that is a lighter orange than other amelanistics.

31

Non-Heritable Alterations of Corn Snake Appearance

All of the sources of variation in corn snake appearance that I have described so far are either clearly heritable (the known color and pattern mutations) or are presumed to be heritable (the naturally occurring variation). However, appearance can be affected in non-heritable ways. Trivial examples would include scars and deformities caused by injuries or disease. Additionally, there is reason to believe that not all deviations from normal markings are genetic in origin. The acquisition of normal markings in a hatchling corn snake depend not only on a proper genetic blueprint (heritable traits), but also on proper embryonic and post-embryonic development. Abnormal development can have a genetic basis but can also have a non-genetic basis, such as environmental stresses. Because the markings of corn snakes arise before the animal hatches, stresses in embryonic development may potentially produce pattern abnormalities.

To my knowledge, no pattern abnormality in corn snakes has yet been reproducibly shown to be caused by stressful conditions experienced by the embryos. However, there is a precedent in ball pythons (*Python regius*). Ball python eggs that are incubated at cool temperatures can hatch to produce animals with an abnormal irregularly striped pattern instead of the normal rounded blotches (Philippe de Vosjoli, in The General Care and Maintenance of Ball Pythons, 1990, Advanced Vivarium Systems). A similar effect has evidently also been seen in Burmese pythons *(Python molurus bivittatus)*. In my experience with corn snakes, I have observed of couple a of likely instances where abnormally patterned corn snakes have been produced from eggs that were in some way stressed soon after laying. In one instance, a clutch of eggs was unintentionally allowed to become quite desiccated which resulted in the deaths of most of the eggs. The three eggs that survived each hatched out babies that had abnormally narrow blotches (see photo). In another instance, two animals with irregularly patterned longitudinal stripes were produced from eggs that had experienced fungal attack soon after being laid (see photo). One animal was also badly deformed and failed to survive. Although the striped pattern of these animals is reminiscent of the striped and motley mutations (except that the animals from the fungused eggs have a checkered underside), I strongly suspect that the source of this abnormality is not genetic, because none of the many other eggs from the same parents have produced striped animals. In short, it is likely, but not yet proven, that certain stresses that occur to corn snake eggs relatively soon after being laid may bring about abnormal pattern formation.

Another possible non-heritable pattern abnormality that has been seen in corn snakes is piebaldness. A piebald animal is normally colored and patterned except that pigmentation is completely missing is some areas creating large white spots.

Stress-related aberration in a corn snake. Notice the abnormally narrow blotches. Photo by the author.

An irregularly striped corn snake that emerged from an egg attacked by a fungus. Photo by the author.

Bill and Kathy Love have attempted to produce piebald animals from breeding together sibling corn snakes that had one pie bald parent. These breedings were unsuccessful which suggests that the piebald trait that had originally been observed was not genetic in nature.

A particularly striking abnormality that has recently been seen in a corn snake is two-headedness. An adult two headed corn snake was recently obtained by the San Diego Zoo. In addition to corn snakes, the two-headedness trait has been observed in a few other species of snakes as well. Two heads apparently arise when a fertilized egg, or very early embryo, begins to split apart. If the split becomes complete, identical twins will result. If the split is only partial, Siamese twins or partial duplication of body structures (such as a head) may result. This type of abnormality is very unlikely to be heritable.

"Jungle corn", a manmade fertile hybrid between the corn snake *(Elaphe guttata guttata)* and the California kingsnake *(Lampropeltis getulus californiae)*. Photo by Bill Love.

Hybridization of Corn Snakes with Other Snake Species

All the color and pattern variability described so far in this book occurs in animals that are bona fide 100% corn snakes. However, it is possible, under certain conditions, to achieve mating and offspring production between corn snakes and some other related snake species. The first reported example of this was described in 1960 when H. B. Bechtel published an account of offspring produced from the mating of a male corn snake (*Elaphe guttata guttata*) and a female Everglades rat snake (*Elaphe obsoleta rossalleni*) (Copeia, 1960, No. 2, pp. 151-153). The hybrid hatchlings were described as having characteristics intermediate between the characteristics of hatchlings of either single species. Since then, other inter-species hybridizations involving corn snakes have been accomplished, including hybridizations with king snakes (*Lampropeltis getulus*) and gopher snakes (*Pituophis melanoleucus*).

"Gopher corn", a manmade fertile hybrid between the corn snake *(Elaphe guttata guttata)* and a gopher snake *(Pituophis melanoleucus)*. Photo by Bill Love.

determine because recessive genes reveal their presence (by altering the phenotype) only when they are homozygous.

SAMPLE BREEDING OUTCOMES

With a grasp of the above background material, one can begin to consider examples of the inheritance of mutations relevant to corn snakes.

Amelanism is the most common mutation available in corn snakes and will be used as the starting example, but what is said regarding its inheritance will be true of the other single recessive traits described in this book. Amelanism is the lack of the pigment melanin, the normal source of blacks and browns in vertebrates. In corn snakes, amelanism produces red-eyed animals with bright red-orange body coloration that is lacking any black or brown. A candidate gene for causing amelanism in corn snakes is the gene encoding tyrosinase, the enzyme which catalyzes the assembly of melanin pigment. Whatever the precise defect is, amelanism in corn snakes is inherited as a single recessive gene. A corn snake with both copies of the defective gene is amelanistic, and a corn snake with one or both copies of the gene being functional will be normally pigmented.

In order for a corn snake to be amelanistic, both of its parents must either be amelanistic themselves (homozygous for amelanism) or be carriers of the trait (heterozygous for amelanism). Punnett square 1 illustrates the probabilities of different classes of offspring of mating two animals that are each heterozygous for amelanism. The upper case M indicates the normal gene and the presence of Melanin. The lower case m indicates the recessive non-functional form of the gene.

The construction of Punnett squares such as this one requires:

1. The knowledge of what both copies of the gene(s) of interest are (i. e., whether they are normal or mutant).

2. Writing down the possible gamete (egg cells or sperm cells) types produced by each parent. Remember, germ cells are haploid, containing only one copy of any given gene.

3. Combining the germ cell types in all possible combinations to determine the expected classes and frequencies of offspring. Remember that the "expected offspring" in Punnett squares are mere probabilities; the results of actual breedings can be considerably skewed due to chance.

As shown in Punnett square 1, with only one gene being followed, these steps are quite simple:

For step 1- Both parents are stated as heterozygous (Mm).

For step 2- Each parent produces two gamete types- M and m.

For step 3- Three types of offspring (MM, Mm, and mm) are anticipated, in a ratio of 1:2:1, when the different egg and sperm combinations are made.

Half of the offspring of this mating are thus expected to be heterozygous like their parents. One quarter of the offspring are expected to be homozygous normal and the last quarter are expected to be homozygous for amelanism. By eye, 75% should be, on average, normal and 25% should be, on average, amelanistic. Keep in mind that these percentages are expected probabilities, not guarantees of what will happen with any particular clutch of hatching eggs.

The same Punnett square can be used to show the results of crossing an animal heterozygous for amelanism to either class of homozygote (MM normal and mm amelanistic). If the father is the heterozygous animal and the mother is a MM normal, the relevant Punnett square is simply the left column of Punnett square 1. In this cross, the expected progeny will all be normally pigmented and are expected to be 50% Mm heterozygous animals and 50% MM homozygous animals. If the mother is amelanistic (mm), the right column of Punnett square 1 shows the anticipated offspring, 50% heterozygous and 50% mm amelanistics.

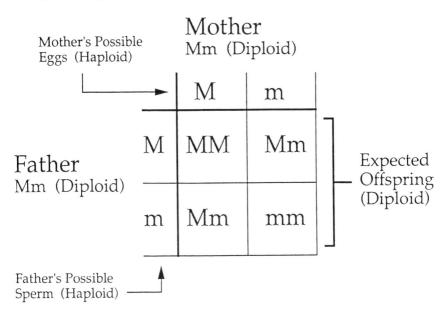

Punnett Square 1. The anticipated offspring from the cross of two corn snakes that are each heterozygous (Mm) for amelanism. mm is the genotype of an amelanistic and MM is the genotype of a homozygous normal.

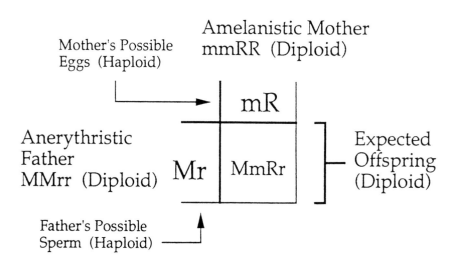

Punnett Square 2. Genotypes of the anticipated offspring from crossing an amelanistic female corn snake to an anerythristic male corn snake. The MmRr offspring will be normal in appearance but genetic carriers of both amelanism and anerythrism.

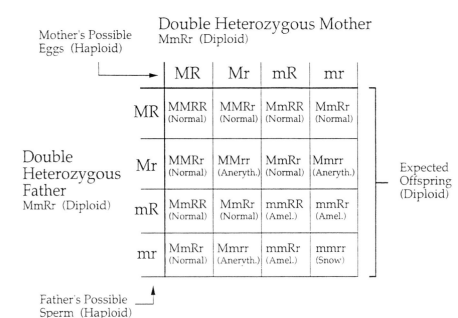

Punnett Square 3. Anticipated outcome of crossing two double heterozygous corn snakes together.

Punnett squares can additionally be used to figure out the anticipated offspring of animals carrying two genetic traits. Say for example, a person wishes to combine amelanism with anerythrism and create a snow corn. Because these two traits involve separate pairs of genes, individual snakes in Punnett squares will always be represented by four letters (two copies each of two genes). Punnett square 2 shows the expected results of mating an amelanistic animal to an anerythristic animal where neither snake is heterozygous for the other trait. An upper case R is used to represent the dominant normal gene that produces red pigment, and a lower case r is used to represent the non-functional red pigment gene.

The steps in making this Punnett square:

Step 1- In each case, part of the genotype can be determined by the phenotype. To be amelanistic, an animal must be mm. To be anerythristic, an animal must be rr. The genotype of the other gene for each animal cannot be judged by looking at the animals. In principle the amelanistic could be mmRR or mmRr (Note: the order of the letters in genotypes is arbitrary as far as meaning is concerned. MmRr=mMRr=rMRm etc..., but the two letters designating the two copies of a given gene are kept together by convention). Likewise, the anerythristic could be MMrr or Mmrr. However, for this example, both are stated as not being carriers of the other trait, and the genotypes are therefore mmRR (amelanistic) and MMrr (anerythristic).

Step 2- Each parent can make only one type of gamete with respect to the two mutations being followed. The mmRR parent makes only mR gametes and the MMrr parent makes only Mr gametes.

Step 3- Single classes of gametes combine to make only a single genotype class of offspring, MmRr.

All offspring of this mating are heterozygous for both amelanism and anerythrism. Because both traits are recessive, these animals will be normally pigmented, but capable of passing on one or both mutations onto their offspring.

A second generation of breeding is necessary to combine amelanism and anerythrism and obtain a snow corn. Punnett square 3 shows the anticipated classes of offspring resulting from the breeding of two siblings of the first cross (offspring of Punnett square 2).

The making of this square:

Step 1- Genotypes of both parents are MmRr.

Step 2- Each parent can produce the same four types of gametes (MR, Mr, mR, and mr). Remember, each gamete will get exactly one copy of each gene, one M

41

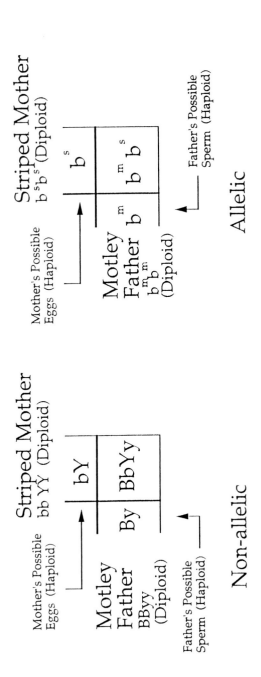

Non-allelic

Striped Mother
bb YŶ (Diploid)

Mother's Possible Eggs (Haploid)

	bY
Motley Father By	BbYy
BByy (Diploid)	

Father's Possible Sperm (Haploid)

Allelic

Striped Mother
$b^s b^s$ (Diploid)

Mother's Possible Eggs (Haploid)

	b^s
Motley Father b^m	$b^m b^s$
$b^m b^s$ (Diploid)	

Father's Possible Sperm (Haploid)

Punnett Square 4 (left). Anticipated offspring of a cross between Striped corn snake and a Motley corn snake if each trait is caused by mutations in different genes. "B" is the dominant (normal) version of the gene involved in striping (bb genotype causes striping) and "Y" is the dominant version of the gene involved in the Motley trait (yy genotype causes Motley trait). The BbYy offspring are expected in this scenario to be normally patterned.

Punnett Square 5 (right). Anticipated offspring of the same cross if each trait is caused by different alleles of the same gene. "b^s" and "b^m" signify the alleles for Striping and Motley, respectively. The normal (wild-type) allele "B" is not present in either of the parents or in the offspring. The pattern phenotype of the offspring in this scenario is difficult to predict, but could be motley or intermediate between motley and striped.

(M or m) and one R (R or r).

Step 3- Combining all possible gamete types results in a 4 X 4 square. A little tedious to fill in, but basically straightforward.

Nine of the sixteen "offspring" in this Punnett square contain one or more normal copies (upper case letters) of both genes and would be normally pigmented despite having any of four different genotypes. Similarly, 4/16 of the expected offspring are homozygous for amelanism (mm) and 4/16 are homozygous for anerythrism (rr). These two groups overlap in 1/16 to produce the double homozygous animal (mmrr) that is missing both pigments (snow corn). The ratio of normal : amelanistic : anerythristic : snow is 9:3:3:1. Crossing one of the double heterozygous parents of Punnett square 3 with a snow corn will produce the four color varieties in equal numbers (a ratio of 1:1:1:1).

ALLELES

An allele is simply a particular "version" of a gene. A corn snake that is heterozygous for amelanism would carry two different alleles (one mutant and the other wild-type) of the gene involved in the amelanism trait. Although an individual diploid organism can carry at most two different alleles of any given gene, there can be any number of different alleles for any given gene in the population of a species taken as a whole. A well known example of this from humans is the ABO blood type system. Individual people may carry any two of the three alleles, A, B, or O, but cannot carry all three.

Although there are, as yet, no established instances of corn snake genes with multiple alleles, there is at least one potential instance. The motley and striped mutations both eliminate the ventral pattern and both cause a tendency for blotches to run together into longitudinal stripes. The motley and striping mutations are therefore candidates to be different alleles of the same gene in spite of the fact that they produce unmistakably different patterns.

The two alternative scenarios for the inheritance of the motley and striping mutations (two totally different genes versus two different alleles of the same gene) can be distinguished by breeding experiments. Punnett squares 4 and 5 show the different expectations of the two scenarios. Punnett square 4 shows the anticipated outcome of crossing a motley corn snake to a striped corn snake where the two traits are caused by mutations in two separate genes. Because both parents are assumed to not be carriers of the trait expressed by the other parent, only one kind of gamete can be produced by each parent, and consequently, only one type of offspring will be produced. In this example, the offspring will be heterozygous for both traits, and because both traits are recessive, the offspring should have a completely normal blotched pattern. Punnett square 5 shows the anticipated outcome if motley and striping are caused by different mutant alleles of the same gene. The three hypothetical alleles could be designated: B (blotched, which is the dominant allele), b^m (motley), and b^s (striped). If both parents are homozygous for their particular allele, only one offspring class can be produced, the $b^m b^s$ heterozygote. The absence of the dominant B allele in these offspring leads to the prediction that the offspring will have an abnormal pattern, perhaps intermediate between typical motley and striped corn snakes, or perhaps like typical motley corn snakes (the motley mutation would most resemble the dominant blotched condition and might therefore be dominant over striping). The actual answer to whether motley and striped are alleles of the same gene or different genes altogether has yet to be determined as no one has, at the time of this writing, crossed the two strains together.

Another example of mutations that could, at least in principal, be caused by different alleles of the same gene involves hypomelanism and amelanism, as both of these mutations affect the same thing, namely the amount of the pigment melanin present in the skin. In this case, however, the two mutations almost certainly involve different genes as a cross that I made between a hypomelanistic corn snake and a corn snake heterozygous for amelanism produced only normal looking offspring, an outcome inconsistent with the the two traits being allelic.

INBREEDING
Inbreeding refers to the breeding together of closely related individuals. The result of inbreeding are offspring that are much more likely to be homozygous for rare recessive mutations than would offspring from randomly mated parents. A numerical example will illustrate the tremendous ability of inbreeding to "expose" recessive mutations. Say that the frequency of occurrence of amelanism in a wild population of corn snakes is one animal in 10,000. Only animals that are homozygous for amelanism are seen as mutants, but many other individuals in the population would be expected to be heterozygous silent carriers of the amelanism trait. In a randomly mating population, the expected frequency of a recessive gene is the square root of the frequency of the observable frequency of homozygotes. In the example above, approximately one animal in 100 is expected to be a carrier of the amelanism gene when amelanistic individuals are present at the level of 1 in 10,000. The mutant *gene* for a recessive trait such as amelanism is thus much more frequent than homozygous individuals that express the mutation. In our example, a corn snake that is heterozygous for amelanism will have a 1 % chance of mating with another individual that is a carrier of amelanism if mating occurs at random. However, if the same heterozygous individual breeds with its own sibling, the chance of the sibling also being heterozygous is 50 % (assuming only one parent carries the amelanism gene and that parent carries it in the heterozygous state, the most likely situation when the mutant gene is uncommon). The brother-sister inbreeding in this example thereby produces a 50 fold increase in the likelihood of seeing amelanistic offspring compared to what would be expected with random breeding.

BENEFITS FROM INBREEDING

The ability of inbreeding to enhance the chances of producing individuals homozygous for rare mutations has two useful applications for snake breeders. First, inbreeding is virtually essential to reproduce newly discovered mutations. Some of the known corn snake mutations are probably descendants of a single original animal that expressed the mutant trait. Only through the inbreeding of the original mutant individual, or its descendants, is it feasible to produce more animals expressing the mutant trait. Most of the inbreeding that is done with corn snakes is done for this reason. The second, related, utility of inbreeding is its potential usefulness in discovering new mutations in the first place. Undoubtedly, interesting mutations are probably present, but yet undetected, in corn snakes currently being kept in captivity. Only inbreeding is likely to uncover them.

THE COSTS OF INBREEDING

Though inbreeding has important uses, it also has potentially important draw-backs. Just as inbreeding greatly increases the likelihood of exposing interesting recessive mutations, it also greatly increases the likelihood of simultaneously exposing harmful recessive mutations. The effects of harmful mutations can vary enormously and include major problems such as deformity, embryonic death, sterility, decreased resistance to disease, and shorter life span as well as minor problems such as behavioral quirks or slight physical abnormalities. It should be noted, however, that not all problems that hatchling corn snakes may be afflicted with are due to inbreeding. Many, probably most, are birth defects that can occur for a number of reasons including improper conditions during egg incubation.

The effects that inbreeding produces tend to vary depending upon how many generations of inbreeding have occurred. With minimal inbreeding, probably the sort most relevant to corn snakes, variation among offspring will still be high, and most offspring will probably not be appreciably negatively affected by the inbreeding. Because of the uncovering of previously hidden recessive mutations, the first generation or two of inbred animals may actually appear to be more variable than the offspring of randomly mated animals. An example of this was seen with the color variation in the offspring of the double heterozygous siblings in Punnett square 5. Similarly, if both parents carry a harmful mutation, most offspring may be fine, but a minority of the offspring will be afflicted with the problems caused by being homozygous for the mutation. If that mutation is lethal when homozygous, then a fraction of the eggs can be expected to simply fail to hatch. Basically, the extent of problems from a modest amount of inbreeding will be variable and impossible to predict in advance.

With each additional generation of inbreeding, offspring will become more and more alike in every respect. Ironically, mutations with effects severe enough to prevent survival or reproduction will actually become rarer with multiple genera-tions of inbreeding. Individuals expressing such severe mutations fail to reproduce and genes encoding such severe mutations are thereby filtered out of highly inbred populations. The problems with highly inbred strains tends to be of the more subtle variety. Though largely missing the most severe mutations, they may have become homozygous for alleles of genes that leave them not quite as healthy and vigorous as non-inbred animals.

For corn snakes, the issue of inbreeding becomes important if you are interested in keeping individuals expressing some of the color and pattern mutations. The rarer mutant forms, and combinations of more than one mutation are probably more likely to be the product of recent inbreeding than are normal corn snakes or the most common mutant forms such as amelanistics. If you intend to purchase corn snakes of a strain that is inbred, and if you are obtaining animals directly from the breeder, inquire about the health and fertility of the parents and any problems that may have been observed with the strain. If you have a choice of animals, and if other factors (e. g., appearance) are equal, choose individuals that seem to have had less inbreeding. In short, be aware that inbreeding can raise the risks of problems, but don't let inbreeding necessarily interfere with what you would like to get.

Glossary of Corn Snake Varieties

Albino. Common name for amelanistics.

Amelanistic. Corn snakes lacking black pigment in both skin and eyes as a result of a mutation. Brightly colored red and orange.

Anerythristic. Corn snakes that lack red pigment as a result of mutation. Primarily marked with greys.

Black albino. Name occasionally used for anerythristic corn snakes.

Blood Red. An inbred strain of corn snakes characterized by a rather solid, dark red-orange coloration and an abnormal belly pattern.

Candy corn. A high contrast amelanistic with deep red-orange blotches on a whitish ground color.

Ghost. Tannish corn snakes that are both hypomelanistic and anerythristic.

Great Plains rat snake. The brown and grey western subspecies of the corn snake.

Hypomelanistic. Corn snakes with black pigmentation greatly diminished but not absent. True hypomelanistics are the result of a recessive mutation.

Melanistic. Name occasionally used erroneously for anerythristic corn snakes. True melanistic animals are typically solid black.

Miami phase. Corn snakes of the eastern subspecies that are grey with red-orange blotches.

Motley. Corn snakes with a mutation that results in irregularities in the pattern of the dorsal blotches.

Okeetee. Name sometimes given to corn snakes of the eastern subspecies that are particularly orange in color.

Red albino. Name sometimes used for amelanistic corn snakes.

47

Rosy rat snake. Corn snakes from the lower Florida Keys. Previously thought to have been a third subspecies of the corn snake because of their minimal amount of black coloration both dorsally and ventrally.

Snow. Whitish corn snakes that are the result of a combination of the amelanistic and anerythristic mutations.

Striped. Corn snakes with longitudinal stripes running down the back instead of the normal blotched pattern. Striping is caused by a recessive mutation.

White albino. Name sometimes used for snow corn snakes.

Zigzag. Variably patterned animals that often have their dorsal blotches connected together in a way that results in a rather zigzag-like pattern.

WANTED!

I would be interested in receiving information about new variations of corn snake in order to be best prepared for a future edition of this book. If you are aware of any new variants, feel free to contact me through AVS.

Michael McEachern
c/o Advanced Vivarium Systems
P.O. Box 408
Lakeside, California 92040